PRAISE FOR *ZOM-FAM*

A CBC Best Book of Poetry
A *Globe and Mail* Best Debut
QWF Concordia University First Book Prize Finalist

This is a story about being and becoming, about creating vocabularies for yourself and stepping into them as you would a home. La Mackerel has wrought such a vocabulary for this collection, one that is tender and honest, that defies the boundaries of the English language.
— *Canthius*

This poetry collection tells a new story of Mauritius's history, one that includes and celebrates the queer and trans stories that helped shape the island's history.
— CBC Books

ZOM-FAM is uplifted by Kama La Mackerel's years of intimate stage performance. They are an interdisciplinary artist who unquestionably knows how to summon their audience's close and venerated attention. These long-form poems offer highly engaged and unique modes of storytelling. Even on the page, one can hear La Mackerel's arresting anaphora, breathy rhythms and varied lyrical tempo; one can see their abundance of sensory imagery and motifs of Mauritian place making. Both enchanting and exacting, these poems are, indeed, blessed with the femme divine.
— Amber Dawn, author of *How Poetry Saved My Life: A Hustler's Memoir*

Kama subverts the coming of age story into radiant poetry, brimming with ritual, ancestry and feminine power. *ZOM-FAM* is the book I've been eagerly waiting for.
— Vivek Shraya, author of *even this page is white* and *I'm Afraid of Men*

In *ZOM-FAM*, Kama La Mackerel spins wondrous, powerful stories into a poetry that fills. There is so much pleasure in these pages, and much contemplation too ... about the things that sometimes make us feel in flux: gender, race, colonialism, kinship. A feat in artistry, their poetic touch here is both light and knowing. This work will sing in my body and imagination for a long time. Probably forever.
— Jenny Heijun Wills, author of *Older Sister. Not Necessarily Related. A Memoir*

Kama La Mackerel's *ZOM-FAM* is a historic and important book— and a triumph. *ZOM-FAM* reminded me of things I needed to remember, and taught me things I needed to know. La Mackerel's re-memory of indentured femme travels across the kala pani to make a home brick by brick, their invocations and re-imaginings of divine Mauritian femme intimacies, secrets, mysteries, their recounting of colonial scars and their telling of the alchemy of their reject are crucially and beautifully told. La Mackerel writes with the whisper and shout of a genius storyteller, words that you won't soon forget.
— Leah Lakshmi Piepzna-Samarasinha, author of *Tonguebreaker*, *Dirty River*, *Care Work*, co-editor of *Beyond Survival*

ZOM-FAM

ZOM-FAM

Poems

Kama La Mackerel

METONYMY PRESS

Montreal, Quebec

First edition
Second printing - 2021
Printed in Quebec, Canada by Imprimerie Gauvin
ISBN: 978-1-9990588-4-5 (paperback)
ISBN: 978-1-9990588-6-9 (electronic book)

Metonymy Press
PO Box 143 BP Saint Dominique
Montreal, QC H2S 3K6
Canada

Cover design by Kai Yun Ching and Aun Li
Poetry editing by Amber Dawn
Mauritian Creole editing by Gaëlle Tossé

Earlier versions of "the invocation" and "gran-dimounn" were published in *Glitter & Grit: Queer Performance from the Heels on Wheels Femme Galaxy*, Publication Studio (2015)

An earlier version of "twenty years of brick" was published in *We Mark Your Memory: writings from the descendants of indenture*, School of Advanced Study University of London and Commonwealth Writers (2018)

Epigraph excerpted from Kei Miller's *There Is an Anger that Moves*, Carcanet Press Limited (2007)

ZOM-FAM is distributed in Canada by LitDistCo, in the United States by Small Press Distribution and in the United Kingdom, Europe and beyond by Turnaround Publisher Services.

We acknowledge the support of the Canada Council for the Arts.
Nous remercions le Conseil des arts du Canada de son soutien.

 Canada Council   Conseil des arts
for the Arts   du Canada

Library and Archives Canada Cataloguing in Publication

Title: Zom-fam / Kama La Mackerel.
Names: La Mackerel, Kama, 1984- author.
Description: Poems.
Identifiers: Canadiana (print) 20200259997 | Canadiana (ebook) 20200260138 | ISBN 9781999058845 (softcover) | ISBN 9781999058869 (PDF)
Classification: LCC PS8623.A199 Z66 2020 | DDC C811/.6—dc23

for Rita
for Dana-Pakion
& for the lineages they gave birth to

CONTENTS

My love, if we struggle at first
to fit our chests and our legs together
it is only natural. We are different
islands, our borders salted differently.
Love is how our skin breaks against each other,
how we bleed into each other; how we heal.
— Kei Miller

i. the invocation

i invoke our mothers, our grandmothers & our femme ancestries

i invoke the teachers, healers, mentors, caregivers & warrior women of history

i invoke femmes of all genders, bloods, ages, lineages
generations of witches & fighters
who infuse the universe with love, rage & magic

i invoke the dynasties of femmes
who gouged the earth with their bare hands
& planted roots from the seeds of their hunger

i invoke the bloodlines of women & femmes
whose bodies are steep with the darkness of the *kala pani*
whose spirits are awash with the cleansing light of the full moon

i invoke my great-grandmothers
whose unknowing bodies stormed on a ship
from the continent to the island

                              hands tied
                              bodies battered
                              minds resilient

i invoke the deities
who never made it to the shores
their copper flesh an offering
to the creatures that live along the edge   of the unknown
                                                   where ocean becomes sky
                                                   & sky becomes ocean

i invoke the generations
                              who suffered
                              who died
                              who lived
                              who fought
                              who resisted   patriarchy & colonialism
                                                    on sugarcane plantations

i honour my mother, Vimala Devi
nurse, caregiver, teacher, mentor, inspiration
& embodiment of femme power

i honour her mother, Dana-Pakion
whose fortitude knew no bounds
whose story remains

                                untold
                                repressed
                                forgotten
                                chained

                                                    to the silence
                                                    of history

i honour Rita whose womb carried ships
of born & unborn children
brave mother who offered her milk & blood
to quench the inconsolable longing of the aching land

i honour Kathaï, woman of rosewater, saffron, betel leaves & nuts
whose rugged feet walked earth, sand, basalt & burning coal

i honour

            Kamla whose ceremonial fingers enchant
                        the dead & bring their spirits back to life

            Ouma whose visions speak
                        in femme tongues   long forgotten

            Lalita whose salt flows like rivers
                        longing for a sea to call home

            Asha whose ancestral lungs carry curses
                        that quaver like crackles of burning sandalwood

            Devika whose grief is cavernous
                        like a sinuous passage into the night sky

i invoke strength & wisdom from Goddess Kali Mā
                              redeemer of the Universe

        Goddess of Time, Change & Destruction

Goddess with charcoal eyes & a blood tongue

        who cuts patriarchy & wears it as a garland around her neck

Goddess with matted hair & ivory fangs

        who dismembers misogyny & wraps it as a skirt around her waist

        this lineage

                        past, present & future

        the women & femmes

                        who reshape the universe

                        i invoke
                        & i honour

ii. mofinn

bann-la dir ki mo ti ne
enn zour ki ti mofinn
enn zour ki ti soy net

the story goes that i was born on a day that was *mofinn*

on that hot midsummer day
the southeast winds stopped blowing

the sun's burn stagnated high
over the smothered flesh of the island

heat rose

        from the ocean

     in sheets of vapour

             distorting

        the island

          into

             dreamlike

                 landscapes

on that day, the moon was plump & orange
high above the horizon
mirroring the sun against the skin of the sky

geckos gathered on top of banana trees
licked their glazed bulb eyes
clicked their rhythmic tongues

the brittle whistle of their mating dance
an echo swaddled like a shawl
over the bosom of the island

tides churned
fishermen stayed ashore
drinking arak under filao trees
watching the disquiet of the sea
with dread & blood in their eyes

it was *zourne mofinn*

every body felt the ripple of agitation in their heart
prayed away the ill-omened day with bread, salt & water

gran-dimounn—the elders
said it was the retelling of an old sentiment

island bodies are haunted
by the longings of spirits
lost in the *kala pani*

& because we are severed
from the sacred river
we have forgotten the songs
to soothe the torment of the ancestors

so on days like these, *zourne mofinn*
when they sail to us
from the mud of the ocean
our bodies bruise & brood

my mother

       a nurse
       in the tenth lunar cycle
       of her pregnancy
       working her day shift
       at the hospital

felt her ribcage outstretch like mangrove roots
into the swelled waters of her belly

she heard the voice of her dead mother
thin like smoke in her right ear

                  & she knew the time had come

she breathed deeply
asked Durga Mā & *Lavierz Nwar* to protect her
& filled out the paperwork to admit herself into hospital

                         an hour later
                         i breathed
                         my first breath

the great-grand-aunt, who was the oldest member of the family
was immediately brought in to see me

a full set of hair

two eyes   two ears

two arms   two feet

a small flat nose   a belly button

&

a

penis

"li paret enn zoli baba
selman get ki zour li'nn ne
enn zour mofinn
ki ou pou fer si so koko pike
al get swami
dimann li ki pou fer pou
beni zanfan-la"

13

my father woke up before sunrise the next morning
he shaved, showered
applied a smear of *vibhuti* on his forehead

he grabbed the platter of offerings
he had prepared the night before

> bananas, coconut, milk
> rosewater, saffron, marigolds
> honey, camphor, *gato koko*

& rushed to the Mariammen kovil

he passed the peacocks perched on mango trees
roosting in the precinct of the temple

he entered the courtyard
removed his sandals
rinsed his feet
circled the temple three times
breathed deeply
                    & finally stepped across the doorway

as the first light of the day
washed over the sculpted
eyes of a thousand & one gods

he bowed to each one of them
praying praying
praying praying
they'd protect me from the towers
of *mofinn* looming over my destiny

when he was done breaking coconuts
lighting sandalwood
dropping money in donation jars
praying praying
praying praying
so the pantheon would shed light
onto the crevices of my kismet

he fell to his knees & exhaled

"*ayooooooooooooooooswamiiiiiiiiiiiiii*
voiceofknowledgevoiceofwisdom

mo garson inn ne yer
zis dan ler mofinn

is there anything we can do
to bless the child"

swami looked at my father with luminous eyes
striped with ash, compassion & ceremony

he burnt camphor on a copper platter
whirled it six times around the Goddess

folded in pleats of red & yellow silk
seated in her chariot of golden snakes

he placed a garland of 108 limes around her head
nestled under her crown of lotus petals

he snapped his fingers three times at her side
lodged blue hortensias between her ears & her shoulders

with Mariammen's blessing & an earthen lamp
swami sat on the ground
opened his books & his charts

the entire cosmos with

————dots————lines————numbers————sanskrit————

spread

       with galaxies

           known &
           unknown

in the shape of travelling

           stars

       suns

     & moons

           fated &
           unfated

                it was all written

                      my destiny

"tuesday
born at 2:45pm
born in Pamplemousse"

swami's thick fingers pelted like meteors
over the swath of charts, scores, figures

.veins of the universe

silhouetted into vedic chants

tabulated into equations

refigured into mantras

that slipped from under his tongue

as his eyes orbited 108 times

over & around my destiny

taking a deep breath
swami bloated his belly
like that of Ganapati

"KAAAA
his name shall start with KAAAA
& shall comprise only two syllables"

my father knelt down
his hands folded in prayer
small & humble
at the feet of swami
voiceofknowledgevoiceofwisdom

he stooped his forehead to the ground
his body a platter of gratitude
his heart a single flower
searching for light
amongst a field of frangipanis
his lips a never-ending breath
touched by the grace
of a thousand & one gods

prostrate, he looked up
into the eyes of Mariammen

"KAAA"

as he said it out loud for the very first time
my father's skin felt awash in a sea of *vibhuti*
his hairs arose in whirls
        milky
        delicate
        earthy
like an island of smoke
soaring over a boundless primeval ocean

he looked deep into the eyes of Mariammen

in her chiselled, penetrating gaze
he saw soft skin, curly hair

kohl-outlined playful eyes
a black *pottu* on a tender forehead
a vision of the daughter
he had always wished for, longed for

        time stood still
        perched on the edges of his vision
        ephemeral like wrinkled waves of lilac haze

my father chanted prayers
in a language he could not even understand
but echoed purity in the temple of his soul

he trusted his vision was a good omen
a message from Mariammen he'd later have to decipher
satisfied he had broken
the shadow of *mofinn*
lurking over my destiny

he grabbed his platter of offerings
dropped more money in donation jars
walked backwards towards the doorway of the temple
found his sandals
& made his way to the city of Port-Louis
eager to name his newborn child

my father held on to the KAAA in his hands
like a precious gift
        a healing syllable
        an occult melody
        a miraculous remedy
until he reached the civil status office

he got me a birth certificate
without consulting anyone—not even my mother

                        he named me Kama

for years after that, whenever i asked my parents how i got my name
no one told me that i was born on *zourne mofinn*

my father simply said
he had read an article in Reader's Digest
where he learnt that in indian mythology
Kāma is the God of Love
a deity armed with a bow
made of sugarcane stalk
a bowstring made of a line of bees
& arrows tipped with five flowers

                    & he thought

                                        it was beautiful

he could never explain to me why the names of the boys & men
in the family are

Sourensen
Karlsen
Cadressen
Coumaren
Krishnen
Vallen
Krissen
Vissen

& the names of the girls & women
in the family are

Youmila
Shameela
Brinda
Yovana
Yanka
Vanessa
Priyanka
Sapna

& the name that became mine   Kama

iii. twenty years of brick

in 1986, almost two decades post-independence

on an island where the colonial carcasses of power
   have been transferred to a displaced & broken people

where a starved population feeds on opportunism
   like dregs of banana wine in the hollow of a bottle

in 1986, on an island where political & economic insecurity
   trembles like magma in the veins between

         kreol   *laskar*   *malbar*   *madras*

                    ti-nasion   *gran-nasion*

where the smell of collective trauma
   hangs like dried octopus under the sun

my parents each hold a child in one arm

                & using their free hand

                              they sign

grandchildren of *girmitiyas*—"the agreement people"
            inheritors of a corrupt
            british understanding of a contract
                              spawned from thumbprints
                              on faithless documents
                              like passports in a language
                              they did not even understand

my parents sign on a piece of paper

            indentured muscle memory
            works its black ink
            into the tip of the pen

                  doubt & fear shake their souls
                  peace & redemption settle their fingers

my parents sign

            their first mortgage
            the first mortgage in family history
            land-owning-mortgage
            french-speaking-mortgage
            government-job-mortgage
            colour-tv-mortgage
            maybe-even-a-car-someday-mortgage

on the island of emancipation
      where power is up for grabs
            dreams are clouded
                  with ancestral hopes
                        broken promises
                              artifacts made of gold
                                    can be found under rocks
                                          if you dig
                                          long enough
                                          hard enough

or if your cousin is married
to a minister's daughter
or if you serve whiskey
lamb biryani
& *rasgullas*
in a thick envelope
to the fat-bellied man
in a blue shirt

the island is parched
like dried mud on a sandbank

                  thirsting for revenge
                  for poetic justice that reeks like rust

                  ti-dimounn, gran-dimounn
                  sakenn tant zot sans

in 1986, my parents absolve themselves from plantation heritage
signing themselves into a lifetime of repayment
their consent redeeming ancestral bonds

they buy a piece of land on which leans

                a room

                          an outdoors toilet
                          an outdoors kitchen

formerly the residence of *bann domestik*
servants, on the edge of white people property

they fill the room with   a bed, two mattresses
                     a cupboard, two boxes
                     of tableware, an iron
                     a sewing machine
                     enough faith & commitment

to keep our four bodies warm as we sleep
under this leaking roof we don't dare call ours

over the next twenty years

               this roof

                       will stretch itself

                              over our heads

                            like new constellations
                        written to bear witness
                 to the whispers of my parents
                   as they brainstorm, budget
                       scheme, plot, plan
                       late into the night

by 1990   we have a living room
                 & an extra bedroom
                 that my brother & i share

by 1992   we have an indoors kitchen
                 & an indoors toilet

by 1996   on the cusp of entering adolescence
               i finally inherit my own bedroom

by 2000   we have a separate prayer room
                 where we burn incense sticks
                 to honour our pantheon of gods
                 goddesses, saints, visionaries, prophets

by 2004   all the ground surfaces of the house
                 are carefully tiled
                 & with the leftover tiles
                 my father spends three months
                 conceiving a mosaic on the terrace floor

by 2006   my parents are done
building their house

it took them twenty years

twenty years of bricks
& piles of rock-sand we considered our kin

twenty years of dust
sprayed like a grey film on our skin

twenty years of my father's arched back
& his bruised hands, working

like a saviour he parted the ground underneath our feet
to lay the foundation of our safety

like a god he rose walls from dead earth
to offer shelter to our bodies

surfaces of security
walls of redemption

the alchemy of mixed concrete
the anagram of placed bricks

that he carefully arranged
like scrabble tiles

over this piece of land
he wanted to claim

as ours

every space in   this house
                 our house
                 my house

                                        the house i left behind
                                        the house i ran away from

every space in this house
speaks of my father

the surfaces smell of his cemented hat soaked in sweat
the roof heats up like the burnt skin of his cheeks
the tiled floors slip like his glasses off his nose
the walls have the callused texture of his dried hands like sandpaper

every door frames his pout
        his lower lip pushed forwards
every window reflects the assiduity of his gaze
        the empty depth in the black of his eyes

for twenty years i watched my father build this house

creating his life's work
in the language of men

                        who were forced
                        to cut their tongues

                                        hang them in the wind
                                        like cautionary tales

                                                on sugarcane stalks

                                        their silence
                                        a stout echo

                        haunting
                        haunting

        haunting
        haunting

                                the island
                                like seafoam

for twenty years i watched my father's mechanical body wear itself out
he grew smaller & smaller as the walls around us got higher & higher

my father builtbuilt   builtbuilt
more rooms   a garage
a verandah   an extra bathroom

as the surfaces   spread around us

    so did the distance   between our bodies

        so did the distance   between the words we exchanged

            so did the expanses of the walls   the thickness of the paint
                                                   with which my father
                                                   trapped his feelings
                                                   shielded his heart

his quietude vibrated

      in the sulkiness of his work
      in the ceremonious sipping of his afternoon tea

      in the bitter burn of his right hand against my child face
      whenever he caught me in a dress

      in how he left the radio on all the time
      so he didn't have to hear our voices

      in how he read all the time so he didn't have to engage with us
      pamphlets, flyers, sunday newspapers
      sprawled like leftover food over the dinner table

                      the first time my father visited me in Canada
                          he read the box of salt
                   over lunch during our first meal together

my father lived up to his inheritance
the oldest son in a house with nine kids

i wonder if he dreams in silence at night
extracting his vocal cords
like an empty fish net pulled from water

i wonder if he has visions of his grandmother
crouched in the hold of a ship
the burn of iron under her breast

i wonder if he dreams of his own mother
the day she died of an abortion
after she'd already given birth nine times

my father lived up to his legacy

the legacy of men who were forced
to swallow their tongues
because colonial powers destroyed   people
    lands
    resources
    cultures

        but colonial powers

           also scythed

              the languages

                of love

but this house speaks for him
in an invisible language
only men like him know how to use
the legacy of torn muscles, broken bones, hands at work

                                                            never stopping

in this house is trapped   his life's work
                                  his silence

& in his silence
i hear the voices of our ancestors

our long lineage of displaced, misplaced people
cramped into the house he built
the promised legacy

not a tomb
not a monument
not the gold of the earth
just a place that they can
that we can

finally call   home

iv. existence as gender survivance

when you grow up a queer femme child on a plantation island
there is a story scripted for your body

in this story

age 5, your body knows how to kick a ball
age 9, your body knows not to want or need a hug
age 12, your body knows how to mix concrete
age 14, your body knows how to curse a woman if there isn't enough
sugar in his tea
age 15, your body puffs cigarettes with his friends at the bus station after school
kouma dir enn gran mari
age 17, your body drinks arak under the jackfruit tree at family gatherings
age 20, your body becomes a man who acts like a boy who acts like a man

in this story

your body forges an existence
that dismisses pain
except for the nights
when your body douses his trunk with arak   lava burning
                                                    through his core

as your body roars & rages
shaking the foundations
of the house your body
tried so hard to build

breaking bones
bruising skin
over the sound
of your body's own screaming
until your body
pisses himself
cries to sleep
like the little boy who acts like a man that he is

when you grow up a queer femme child on a plantation island
you quickly learn the urgency of rehearsing

                                        existence as gender survivance

you unwrite the story scripted for your body
you learn to make yourself   discreet enough
                                    small enough
                                    polite enough

so you get to be   the timid child
                                    the helpful child
                                    the studious child
                                    the good child

good because you're quiet

good because you never speak

good because you've learnt

                              to erase yourself

                                                    to disappear

you pocket small change
currencies of acceptance
drops of love
that want you
to quell the femme in you
& you slur

wi mo enn bon zanfan
mo ava fer mo mofinn disparet

you sculpt a soft masculinity
you dilute a brewing femininity
you smuggle desires
into a clandestine body
smother prosody
under your skin

you walk fine lines

    embroidered borders
    boundaries
    etched interstices

archipelagos & dwellings hemmed

        into coastlines
        of being, longing
        belonging

you trace an atlas of illusion

          you carve
          spaces
          for your queerness
          to survive

                  you carve
                  spaces
                  so you can stay
                  alive

you seek refuge   in the silken pleats
                         of your mother's saris

                         in the lyrical fulfillment
                         of pictorial make-believe

                         in the wistful smell
                         of crayons & wood shavings

you wrap yourself in domesticity

                         a blanket
                         of safety

you make yourself small
moulding your figure to fit in nooks
between the fridge & the kitchen door
between the sink & the gas stove

   spaces where you learn
   to slaughter a chicken
   to gut a fish
   to grind garlic, ginger, saffron
   dried chilies & curry leaves
   on a polished slab of black stone

it is in these spaces that you learn
to witness   femme intimacies
                          storytelling
                          gossip
                          sisterhood
                          support
                          softness
                          pointed & sharp
                          like a cooking blade

it is in these spaces you learn
the value of honouring

it is in these spaces you learn
the virtue of worship

it is in these spaces you learn
that resilience is not the silent bruise under your skin
but the hallowed space lodged inside your breastbone

when you grow up a queer femme child on a plantation island
where boys are supposed to act like men
who act like boys who act like men

you conceal your shame like sunset pollen
nested under the folds of rose petals

you dress like a pilgrim
footsteps
on an ocean of burning coal

to prophesy
re-belonging

you lay the foundations for new tongues

                              vocabularies

                              spaces

                              bodies

                                        of existence as gender survivance

v. gran-dimounn

dan mo fami
ena enn zistwar
bann-la kontan rakonte

every time Bolom Ayave, my paternal grandfather
walked the streets of Curepipe
he exclaimed that the first boy of his kin
who would be admitted to the Royal College

would be *gran-dimounn*

the promised child
who'd dig the family
out of plantation heritage

*"gran-dimounn
ki al laba
gran-dimounn"*

the Royal College of Curepipe
known as the Collège Colonial
under the french rule
was an elite boys' secondary school
attended by only the most promising
children of the island

a handful of 150 pupils
selected from a national exam known as the CPE
(Certificate of Primary Education)
for which an entire generation of about 20,000 children sit
when aged just 11

the best are then ranked
from 1 to 3,000—

                    their names & ranks
                    published in local newspapers

                    the first 150 boys get admitted
                    to the Royal College of Curepipe

                    the first 150 girls get admitted
                    to the Queen Elizabeth College

                    each following group of 150 students
                    is then allotted a different secondary school

                    from the most to the least prestigious
                    from the most to the least resourced

                    up to 3,000 boys & 3,000 girls

the 14,000 or so who do not make the cut
try again the following year
or slowly drop out of the education system
to do manual labour

                on a former plantation colony
                the legacy of servitude
                is embedded in

                                    the imagining
                                    & enacting

                                                of independence

when i was 11 years old
i did not perform well enough
in my CPE to be granted
a seat at the Royal College of Curepipe
but i did do well enough
to be granted a seat
in an all-boys catholic school

kolez sin zozef
established by the Frères des Écoles Chrétiennes
where close to 1,000 teenage boys wear
a yellow & green crest
with a black cross over their hearts

ad altiora cum christo

a college known for instilling discipline in young men
who were punished if their white shirts
were not neatly tucked into their khaki shorts

who were forced to eat spoonfuls of french
                                        & catholicism
taught by middle-aged white women
who always had lipstick on
& said *purrrrrr lui* instead of *porlwi*

where under the stern gaze of a discipline master
porn magazines were slipped in envelopes
pressed in the silence
between the national anthem & the daily prayer

where through the language of christ & punishment
men taught boys to become men
to discipline their sweltering hormones

rising in swaths like vapour in the furnace of a factory
rising in scum from the boiling mud of molasses
rising in bullying, blows & blowjobs
in corridors, classrooms & cubicles

ad altiora cum christo
we rise with christ

so, with or without christ

i rose
somehow

i was the first in my family to finish high school
the first to be admitted into university

eighteen, a full scholarship in hand
a suitcase filled with dreams

                        my own
                        those of my parents
                        those of the grandparents i'd never known

i got onto a plane
i left the island
flying over the same tumbling oceans
my ancestors had been forced to cross

                    on a ship

                              a century earlier

here i was, the great   grandchild
                                 dream
                                 redemption
                                 promise

changing the course of history
rewriting the manifest of our destiny
on my way to realize the prophecy
of social upward mobility

my passport of acceptance
into the family

                    queerness re-envisioned as intelligence
                    alterity rewritten as success story
                    a gendered palimpsest
                    now imaged in

                                        distant lands

i remember the anticipation & the anxiety
in my mother's voice
as she would call me every sunday

long distance calls
                    from this small
                    country of mine
                    were expensive

the number of words we could exchange were

        rationed
        calculated
        controlled
        saved up

much like when i was a child

food, water, electricity
every single vegetable
every grain of rice were
                            rationed
                            calculated
                            controlled
                            saved up

every sunday, my mother called me
for eleven minutes

            four minutes
            she allocated
            to my dad

                            seven minutes
                            she claimed
                            for herself

my mother used her seven minutes
to inquire about my health

but more than anything she wanted to know
how i was dealing with my courses

whether i was holding steady with my morale & my grades
whether i would have a chance to complete further studies after my degree
whether i could secure another scholarship
& come back home in a few years

a piece of paper
in hand
that says

the honour of the family

throughout her seven rationed minutes
my mother repeated her mantra
like a prayer for me

*"zis fer to zefor twa
to kone kouma
mo lapriyer for*

stay strong
work hard
& it'll all be fine"

meanwhile she rationed
her own eating habits
fasting to appeal

        the gods

              goddesses

        saints

              visionaries

        prophets

              of her pantheon

monday prayer & fast for Ganapati
deva of wisdom, learning, letters & intellect
the god of beginnings
who would remove obstacles from my path—

> she had some rice *pongal*
> before her sunrise prayers
> & ate nothing until the sun had set

thursday prayer & fast for Shirdi Saï Baba
satguru whose blessings made the journey
across the *kala pani* possible
saint for whom reverence
has run in the lineage of our faith
for the past five generations—

> she drank only water
> throughout the day

friday prayer & fast for Kartikeya
deva of war, devoted child of Shiva & Parvati
who would travel on the back of a peacock
to bless me with strength & perseverance—

> she had some rice *pongal*
> before her morning prayers
> & ate nothing
> until she finished her evening prayers

sunday prayer & fast for Surya
deva of daylight & the rising sun
who would dispel the darkness in my birth charts—

> she ate nothing
> for the first half of the day

my mother's days were moulded
in rituals of worship
& her nights were fragmented
in worn-out dreams

her dreams hummed
                like the engine
of a sugarcane factory
                as it worked day & night
to produce more
                & more & more
for one extra rupee
                for two extra rupees
for three extra rupees
                her dreams smelt thick
like the lingering scent
                of molasses fogging
our encampment
                as the sugarcane
got crushed
                the stout liquid
oozed out
                & glazed
our mornings
                our evenings
with its smell
                an uninvited guest
not knocking on our door
                entered the intimacy
of our home, clung
                to our walls
our furniture
                our clothes
our skin, our hair

her dreams tasted
   of coarse sugar greased
in the long-running mill
   that controlled
the rhythm & beat
   of our hearts
that disciplined
   the oxygen coming in
& out of our lungs
   that governed
our every word
   our every thought
our every mind
   our every self

      colonized just as much
      as the bodies of our ancestors
      who were dragged onto this ship

ripped from   their land
        their family
        their culture

          to come down to the island

where they worked in fields

      in the unrelenting sun

         from dawn to dusk
         from day to night
from the tops of their burnt
sweat-parched heads

      to the tips of their coarse fingers

         where the only sensation
         known to them was

            pain

my father on the other hand
used his four rationed minutes
to ask me about the weather
about what i had eaten for dinner
about my friends (whom he didn't even know)

or he would tell me something
seemingly relevant or interesting
he had read in the local newspapers
like Ananda Devi published a new novel
like Mauritius held its first pride parade

or he'd remind me that Kofi Annan went to MIT
Barack Obama went to Harvard
Malala just started a degree at Oxford

he collected information about ivy leagues
like marigolds threaded into a garland
he wanted to place around my neck

every once in a while
he would throw in a word
of encouragement
wishing me luck for my exams
or giving me academic advice
that he had picked up from Reader's Digest

even though he never directly asked me   about myself
he skillfully created a vocabulary
around newspaper trivia
to show me that he cares

between the fine print of articles
read like the words of god
the prayers, rituals, fasts
desires & dreams—

      my own
      those of my parents
      those of the grandparents i'd never known

i tried to unwrite the crossing of our lineage
except i could not escape
the remembrance of my own body

for my family, i became big
they call me *gran-dimounn*

except i could never tell them

how
small
i felt

within the confines of these ivory towers
tall walls like chimneys of sugarcane factories
built over the broken bodies of people

        like me
        like them
        like us

vi. your body is the ocean

to lekor se to lakaz
to lekor se enn zil

to lekor se to lakaz
to lekor se losean

take a deep breath
expand your timid lungs
as wide as you can

breathe in
   the salty air of the island
   the humidity of Curepipe
   the musky fumes of Saint-Julien

satiate your chest
       with the gentleness of moss
       the golden chimes of hope
       inflate your belly like

         red
         blue
         yellow
         green
         balloons
         rising
         to the sky
         kan zour
         lindepandans

extend this breath
      to the deepest
      chambers in your body

the unknown spaces
      where there are stories hidden
      that you are yet to discover

like the unsent letters you wrote
      wrapped in tender-green fabric & coconut rope
      hidden under the pile of clothes in your closet

                            breathe deep

& breathe out

> breathe out the amber of life
> breathe out the flame of resilience
> breathe out the heat of forbearance

> breathe out the swell of light
> that will guide you through
> nights, dark & endless
> like the *kala pani*

> *you are the Child of survivance*

your skin will spread & rise
> stretched out vertically
> like a sculpture
> a monument
> demanding to exist
> to be recognized
> to occupy space

your bones will mould themselves
> in a chrysalis of fortitude
> collecting strength from the compost of the earth
> learning not to rust, not to crumble, not to break
> under the wilting weight of adulthood

your hair will sprout & grow
> in length, in strength, in thickness, in pride
> curls like dark snakes in an occult dream will
> bounce & twirl like a proud prophecy
> proclaiming august visions
> of the past & the future to the winds

put a hand
     to your chest
     listen to the cadence
in your ribcage
     running wild
     & feverish
like horses
     stomping across
     the Champs-de-Mars
feel the swelling of life
     under your skin
     the ripple of blood
flowing saltwater
     lapping along
     the coastlines
of your body

voices refusing
     to be silent
songs refusing
     to disappear
screams demanding
     their oscillation
be heard in the ripples
     of the ocean

there will be pain
deep pain

that will settle
like sediment in your marrow

that will calcify
like sandstone in your throat

that will fossilize
like mud on your tongue

you will find ways

to truncate
your roots
from memory

to escape
yourself
& others

catching planes & trains
hiding in the safety
of metal boxes

stretching the distance

between

you
you
you
you

& your home
& your island
& your body
& your pain

no matter the borders, fences, walls
masses of lands, bodies of water you put

       between

you   & your home
you   & your island
you   & your body

               the pain
            is something
        you just can't
      leave behind
    you will drag
   its festering weight
halfway across the globe
in a heavy
invisible
suitcase
grief
the size
of your ribcage
heartache
the length
of your spine
a burden
you just can't
leave behind

the worst thing that could happen to you
    will happen to you

the best thing that could happen to you
will also happen to you

so make friends with your bones
  soak them overnight in coconut oil
wrap them in banana leaves
  polish them under the moonlight

rub salt inside of your pores
  encrust the cracks in your skin
your scars & imperfections
  dried fruit crystallized
on a copper platter
  yielded to *surya*
for preservation

offer your earthy armour
to the open skies

let the burn of salt
purify
your pain

                the rawness of tears
                purge
                your wounds

                                            the churn of waves
                                            cleanse
                                            your island body

                        dig mountains
                        with the edges
                        of your hipbones

            sculpt temples
            from the softness
            of your lips

                                            make homes
                                            for the sacredness
                                            of your stories

your body is home
your body is an island

your body is home
your body is the ocean

you are the Child of lineages
    of ceremonial femmes
who dreamt you up
    reshaped the universe
so they could give birth

    to you

    a promise
       celebration
offering
    pact
omen
    earthen lamp
on your ancestors' altar
    molten lava exploding
in the belly of a volcano
    roaring fire at sunset
echoes of
    ravann maravann triang
krakman dibwa ki ape brile
    lafime ki pe monte lao
kot nou bann zanset
    kot nou al rod nou bann zistwar
bann gran-dimounn
    ki ti refiz disparet
bann zom-fam
    ki'nn kontinie
viv dan nou leker
    ki'nn kontinie
viv dan nou lavenn

there are languages you do not yet speak
words you do not yet know
music you have never heard
magic you have never felt

but you will learn that they have been
                                 with you
                                 within you
                                 all this time

which is why i am here to tell you

                 Child

                 you will not learn
                 to love yourself

                 but i am learning
                 to love you

vii. zom-fam

when i tell my mother that i am trans
her lips wobble a minor tremor
but her silence does not span
the three decades of my life

she smiles with compassion
she speaks her golden heart—
soft, warm, welcoming

her eyes cast a resilient glow
she does not need to tell me about our history
our lineage is one

        of silence

                that we weave

      in between

                our intimacies

but her body
her brown, exhausted body
speaks of her childhood

i see in her old eyes
the grimy streets of Port-Louis
grey, dusty, stifling under the burning sun

i see in the drooping ridges around her cheeks
the cold embrace of banyan trees
when the summer heat became too heavy to bear

i see in the shakiness of her eyelids
melted tar gluing itself
to her eight-year-old feet—

        in the streets of the capital
        poverty was a sticky business
        particles of blackness stained
        the virtuous skin of childhood

i see in my mother's shiny forehead
in the beads of sweat
that place themselves evenly on her skin

a child pushing a cart—

  ounnde, poutou, adourson, soooo
  ounnde, poutou, adourson, soooo

those sweets that her godmother made diligently
with freshly crushed coconut & ground rice
that she'd push
      in a cart
          every single day
             of her life
                from Plaine-Verte
                  all the way to Cité Sainte-Croix

                ounnde, poutou, adourson, soooo
                ounnde, poutou, adourson, soooo

        ounnde, poutou, adourson, soooo
        ounnde, poutou, adourson, soooo

when i look deep into the battered trenches
under my mother's eyes
i see copper coins shifting hands

churchgoers, beggars
children, sex workers
faithful & unfaithful

unwrapping
round coconut
ground rice sweets
from the humidity of newspapers

dipped into hot black tea

an everyday ritual
of my mother's childhood
in Cité Sainte-Croix

when i tell my mother that i am trans
her withered hands shake
like dried twigs forgotten by history
but her silence does not span
the three decades of my life

she tells me

"pa trakase twa Kama, to kone
dimounn kouma twa
tou letan ti ena sa"

she tells me that we come from a history & a culture
where women-men
& men-women

                                    have always existed

that people like me are present
in our myths & our religions
for as long as she can remember

vie dimounn, the elders
spoke of the men-women
& the women-men

her eyes mirror phantom images
            lucent narratives line her haunted lips
she whispers into the soles of my feet
            that she vaguely remembers an old relative
who lived close-by... when she was a child...
            who was... who was... "of my kind..."

but she immediately
closes her heart
fetters her lungs
stitches her throat
with a filament of concealment

she threads the unspoken between our bodies
because our lineage is one

        of silence

                that we weave

      in between

              our intimacies

every day since, i dream of my mother's childhood
i dream of this old relative who was... "of my kind..."

            sometimes i call him Pajani

sometimes i call him Deva Kumar

                sometimes i call her Badet

sometimes i call her Neela

but most of the time i call her Kumkum

i dream of Kumkum with round shoulders
a blood-red bindi on her forehead
a glint of gold hanging over the edge of her pointed nose
      raven curly hair, a tad too greasy
      but that still bounces up & down the nape of her neck
      as she walks in the morning sun

    Kumkum wears plain cotton kurtas
      that she haggles in the markets of Plaine-Verte
& if she ever gets invited to a wedding
she adorns herself of her most prized garment
      a brocaded red salwar kameez
      that wraps her rotund body
      like the heavy skin of syrupy litchi

Kumkum eats rice, dal & pickles during the week
& on weekends, she treats herself to some dried, salted fish
cooked with onions, fresh thyme & tomatoes
      enn bon ti rougay pwason sale
      bien morisien

Kumkum has a radio set
& she listens to the news & *avis de décès* every morning
& hindi songs every evening

    Kumkum rubs coconut oil
    in her thick black hair every friday

Kumkum has a job—

she works in the tobacco factory in the capital city
        with all the poor women whose husbands
        died in obscure wars
        nobody on the island really knows about
        they fought in a faraway british war
        & never came back

on her lunch break
Kumkum does not step out with the other women
to roll tobacco
in small newspaper pieces
that burn their darkened lips
        instead she stays at her workstation
        she sits silently
        & she prays to Goddess Durga Mā
        she prays for protection
        she prays for a good life
        she prays for forgiveness
        she prays for love

when it gets hot in the capital city
Kumkum takes out a white embroidered handkerchief from her purse
& wipes the pearls of sweat from her forehead

        Kumkum likes flower patterns
        she also loves embroidery

on sundays, Kumkum polishes her floor
ek enn bros koko
she brings out her mattress
leans it in the sun
against the mango tree
& beats it with a stick
she winnows her rice & lentils for the week
she makes fruit pickles that she dries on her roof
at the end of the day, she massages her feet
with a slick of warm coconut oil

Kumkum has a lover
but does Kumkum have a lover?

i am not sure yet whether Kumkum has a lover
but this is Kumkum & i dream about her every day

she draws her life like a moving sculpture
a figure ever so ephemeral

becoming & unbecoming herself
with every single one of my dreams

when i tell my mother that i am trans
she does not tell me about Pajani, Deva Kumar, Badet or Neela
she does not even tell me about Kumkum

instead my mother tells me   that   she   is   an   uneducated woman

who feels much pride
that i went to school
that i can read & write
that i speak english & i speak french

she tells me that because of her lack of education
she does not have the words for it
but she understands
that people like me have always existed

she calls me *zom-fam*
which in our local language means man-woman

i take pleasure in being *zom-fam*
a man-woman being neither *zom* nor *fam*
yet being both *zom* & *fam*

navigating a middle passage between being & becoming
an interstice where migrant bodies like mine find their truth
an undefinable space that maps the cartography of my skin
a hyphen that holds & wraps my gendered experience

zom-fam!

        zom-fam!

                                 zom-fam!

    zom-fam!

                            zom-fam!

                                 zom-fam!

                  zom-fam!

   zom-fam!

                      zom-fam!

                                 zom-fam!

               zom-fam!

zom-fam!

                    zom-fam!

                                     zom-fam!

      zom-fam!

                      zom-fam!

                                 zom-fam!

zom-fam!

                    zom-fam!

       zom-fam!

                                 zom-fam!

                      zom-fam!

zom-fam!

                    zom-fam!

                                 zom-fam!

      zom-fam!

                  zom-fam!

                               zom-fam!

zom-fam!

                    zom-fam!

                                 zom-fam!

                zom-fam!

zom-fam!   *zom-fam!*

        zom-fam!

           zom-fam!

   zom-fam!   *zom-fam!*

       zom-fam!

zom-fam!   *zom-fam!*

zom-fam!   *zom-fam!*

     zom-fam!

    zom-fam!   *zom-fam!*

          zom-fam!

      zom-fam!

  zom-fam!   *zom-fam!*

         zom-fam!

      zom-fam!

zom-fam!

      zom-fam!

          zom-fam!

    zom-fam!

       zom-fam!

     zom-fam!   *zom-fam!*

zom-fam!

       zom-fam!

   zom-fam!

         zom-fam!

but my mother tells me
that i shouldn't call myself *zom-fam*
that   she   is   an   uneducated woman
who does not know "those things"

but she-is-happy-is-happy-is-happy
that i have an EDUCATION
that i can call myself TRANS

that i have the words, the language
to describe the mystification of my gender
the longing to tear off my skin
(along with my skin, my birth certificate, my passport
the state-sanctioned papers that dictate my gender)

but deep inside me
there is a voice that speaks
in the uneducated tones of my mother

                              this voice

                   embroiders itself

                              from pore to pore

                   onto the surface

                              of my skin

there is a voice that does not have the words or the vocabulary
but reverberates goodness & music in my body—
my heart beating the drums of my ancestors

there is a voice that did not go to school
does not speak english
does not speak french

        yet echoes wisdom & truth

    in my bloodstream

        like the waves of the oceans

    that witnessed

        the loss of our languages

that voice tells me

      that i do not need an imperial language to define myself
      that i do not need to be trans in english or in french

colonialism has already wrapped itself
like a knot around my vocal cords

& even though our lineage is one

      of silence

              that we weave

      in between

              our intimacies

this voice exists deep within & speaks

like my mother
my grandmother
my great-grandmother
the generations of women & femmes

who fought to keep our language alive
& pass it on from generation to generation

so, mother
i will listen to the voices of our ancestry
femme tongues that dictate i speak out loud

& when i'm done tearing off my skin

(along with my skin, my birth certificate, my passport
the state-sanctioned papers that dictate my gender)

i will take every single piece of torn skin & paper
i will paint them in gold & put them back together
with glistening stars as i so desire

i will build a femme armour

a fierce femme armour

that i will celebrate

an unbreakable   unshakable

object of love

that i will hold together

with respect   & dignity

i will call this armour

zom-fam

when i tell my mother that i am trans
her lips wobble a minor tremor
but her silence does not span the three decades of my life
she does not need to tell me about our history

   our lineage

            is one

                    of a secret language

      a long

                       lost

                                   secret language

     that we weave

                in between our intimacies

                                   zom-fam

viii. towards the femme divine

when i tell my father that i am trans
i see the sun rise in his eyes

he looks at me like dawn
gold fragrance
shiny pebbles
shadow oracles
lodged under cloudy brows

i imagine his gaze when he was my age
on the day he looked up
into the ethereal, sculpted eyes of Mariammen
asking her to   clear my birth charts
                             to sanctify my path

"you see, you were born on *zourne mofinn*
the island breathed fever
our bodies burnt coal

so i went to see swami with a platter of offerings
to seek the blessings of a thousand & one gods

that morning, the Goddess spoke to me
in tongues i could not even understand

but i knew she had answered my prayers
& those of our ancestors"

he says he always believed i would amount to something someday
he prayed i would be diligent about my education

                                    finish high school
                                    go to university
                                    wear a nice suit
                                    work in a bank

he now understands this was not my destiny to fulfill

he tells me my name is Kama

                           the God of Love

because of the miraculous vision
the Goddess had bestowed upon him

this young girl with soft skin, curly hair
playful eyes, outlined in kohl
a *pottu* on her forehead

the daughter he had wished for, longed for

"it took her thirty years
but she finally arrived"

                           yes father, she is here
                           the wild, the fiery, the femme, the sacred

i am a pilgrim with a silver spear
pierced through my tongue

betel leaves between my toes
saffron on the armour of my skin

ash over my devotional eye
a *palkadam* on my head

i travel across oceans
                    i travel across genders

walking across estuaries of coal
          towards Mariammen

                    walking across rivers of blood
                              towards Kali Mā

walking across winds of fire
          towards Durga Mā

                    walking across mountains of honey
                              towards Parvati

          walking across streams of rosewater
                    towards Rita

walking across valleys of smoke
          towards Dana-Pakion

                    walking across oceans of camphor
                              towards Vimala Devi

     walking across islands of salt
          towards the femme divine

ACKNOWLEDGEMENTS

I give thanks for the lands & the waters that have nurtured me & the traditional keepers of the territories where I have lived & loved. I give thanks for the spirits that have guided me in finding my voice, in living my life's purpose. I give thanks for my parents, Vimala Devi & Sorensan, for teaching me the languages of love. I give thanks for the lineages of marginalized writers & creators who paved the way for me to be an artist.

This book has been (re)written over several years through different inter-disciplinary creative processes, before it landed on the page in its current form. My heart is filled with gratitude for the many people & communities who have been part of this journey with me, the artistic mentors & collaborators who have nurtured my process, in particular the creative team that worked on *ZOM-FAM*, the performance.

I am grateful to the P. Lantz Initiative for Excellence in Education and the Arts at McGill University & the Alliance Program of the Montréal, arts interculturels (MAI) for providing me with the resources so I could research & craft this manuscript.

Ashley Fortier, Oliver Pickle & the extended family of Metonymy Press, thank you for seeing me, for seeing the potential in this work & for welcoming me into the Metonymy fold. I could not be more grateful.

Amber Dawn, ceremonial femme who sings in my heart, thank you for accompanying me through this editorial process.

Kai Yun Ching & Aun Li, for the femme labour of love that went into creating this truly beautiful & poetic cover & for loving me in all the shades of the sunset skies.

Reena, my *jahaji-bahain*, my soul-sister, for all the versions of ourselves we gave birth to, for all the oceans we've crossed & the ones we're yet to cross. *mo dedie twa sa liv-la.*

Nedine, my *thangachi*, the honey in my heart, the light in my soul. For this cosmic love, this karmic journey, the many lifetimes past & those yet to come. I am truly blessed to have you as my sister.

Kai Cheng, my love of the red dawn, the blue day, the dark-skinned night & all skies in between. Thank you for choosing me. Thank you for choosing love, always.

jes, for the fire, the water, the salt, the femme armours & the poetry <3

Patrick, my old friend. For all the ways you've held me accountable to my values, to my life's work. For always believing. Thank you.

Magee, Fifi, Annie, Lourdes, Myrna, Devegee, Malor, Naigee, Kamla, Ouma, Lalita, Asha & Devika. Thank you for opening your hearts to me & trusting me to be a keeper of stories.

KAMA LA MACKEREL is a Montreal-based Mauritian-Canadian multi-disciplinary artist, educator, community-arts facilitator and literary translator who works within and across performance, photography, installations, textiles, digital art and literature. They have exhibited and performed their work internationally and their writing in English, French and Kreol has appeared in publications both online and in print. They have lived in far-flung places such as Pune, India and Peterborough, Ontario. *ZOM-FAM* is their first book.

lamackerel.net | @KamaLaMackerel

Photo by Laurence Philomène

ALSO AVAILABLE FROM METONYMY PRESS

A Natural History of Transition
Callum Angus

Dear Black Girls
Shanice Nicole and Kezna Dalz

Dear Twin
Addie Tsai

Little Blue Encyclopedia (for Vivian)
Hazel Jane Plante

nîtisânak
Lindsay Nixon

Lyric Sexology Vol. 1
Trish Salah

Fierce Femmes and Notorious Liars:
A Dangerous Trans Girl's Confabulous Memoir
Kai Cheng Thom

Small Beauty
jiaqing wilson-yang

She Is Sitting in the Night: Re-visioning Thea's Tarot
Oliver Pickle